ISBN-10:1499323999

ISBN-13: 978-1499323993

I AM UNSTOPPABLE

A Guide To Transforming Your Life

Book Design + Branding:
www.pdgbranding.com

Dedication

This book is dedicated to those who have it in their hearts
to start living on purpose and designing their lives.

Florence Gaspard

www.florencegaspard.com

Are you ready to attract the life you want?

Table of Contents

ACKNOWLEDGMENTS

I'm giving my heartfelt thanks to the almighty creator and omniscience presence of the divine in my life. I'm also sending special thanks to my friends and family, whom supported me and continue to support me throughout my journey.

PREFACE

Do you know that every thought you think and every word you speak is an affirmation? We become what we think, feel and speak about, which reflects in how we show up in this world. The word affirmation comes from the Latin word *affirmare*, originally meaning "to make steady, and strengthen. If you ever heard of this phrase" Thoughts become things", you're not alone. However, we cannot rely on our thoughts alone to truly design our lives. What we think doesn't become things; who we are become things, because we are our beliefs. Our thoughts, emotions, and actions are all connected. If we can pause and identify our thoughts, feelings, and behaviors, we will learn important information that could help us move forward with designing our dream lives.

One of the most significant factors that determine our reality is our expectations. What we expect dictates what we believe could happen. Acting upon a thought is translated and create our reality. We have to be very aware of our core beliefs and the vibrations that our energies carry. Using affirmations help with filtering our thoughts and restructuring the dynamic of our beliefs so that we truly begin to live as if nothing is impossible.

Affirmations do indeed strengthen us by helping us believe in the potential of the thing or situation we desire to manifest. When we verbally affirm our dreams and goals we become empowered with a deep sense of reassurance that our words will come to fruition. If you change the way you think about a thing, you'll change the way you feel about it, your attitude towards it, in which your actions and how you approach it will also change. This will lead to changing to a different outcome. A positive affirmation is an initial step of engaging in the transformation process. It's a way of allowing yourself to reconstruct your mind to not only think differently, but also to feel differently and act differently creating a new productive habit(s).

I use affirmations by spending my days visualizing, writing, and commanding my days to see manifest what I desire and showing gratitude for the people, things and my life experiences. There are no empty words, as every word we speak engages energy for us or against us. If you constantly say, "I can't," the energy of your words will go against you. However, if you say "I can!" the universe will provide you with the abilities to do just that and you'll find a way. So create your own future and live up to your potential using affirmations that will transform your decisions resulting in your life transformation.

Positive daily affirmations are simply self-confidence boosting statements you can use to begin building your confidence. Daily affirmations can cover all of the different aspects and areas of your life. Creating affirmations can assist you to connect more with your family, manage work related issues better, or cope in life when things go wrong.

As a transformation therapist, I firmly believe that we attract people, things, and situations into our lives by our energies and vibrations, which is carried by the words we speak, the thoughts we have and the actions we carry out. If we strip everything back to the basics, everything is energy. The universe is simply responding to the energy we carry. I also rely on my spirituality to guide me through life. By focusing on my spiritual presence, it helps strengthen my core foundation and play a significant role in how I show up in the world, because I'm showing up in the authentic essence of I am. I want you to be more aware about the energy you are sending out. You can get a clue of what energy you are sending by looking and paying attention to where you are and what is happening in your life. Ask yourself these questions; do you treat yourself very well? For example, "Do you break promises to yourself? Do you speak up when things do not feel right with you? Or, do you set clear boundaries with others? Are you judgmental of others, or fear judgment from others? Are you struggling financially? Are you settling where you are, knowing there's better? You answers to these questions can help you figure out if the vibration you are sending actually match what you want to send.

Within these pages, you'll learn how all things, wanted and unwanted, are brought to you by powerful natural laws to include the Law of Abundance and Attraction. You'll learn how to use these Laws deliberately in your daily life. This book is complete with tips, activities, and affirmations you can use to start designing your dreams. Remember, not to be discouraged by any setbacks you experience, as you evolve. As you become more skilful at setting your intentions and being more in alignment with the life you want to create as your life will become easier to shape.

"I AM A Divine Manifestation of the Most High"

The Law of Attraction allows what you need to fall into place. Right about now, you are attracting people, jobs, situations, and relationships to you. Science shows us that everything is made up of energy. It's infinite and in everything, including us. We are divine energy. Divine Energy is the source of all abundance. Our needs and desires arise from the deep level of our spirits. Having that knowledge is the greatest wisdom we can possess. The significance of knowing this is for us to wake us up, and realize that we attract those things and people we are a vibrational match with. In other words, "your vibe attracts your tribe and the ride you get in life".

Your mood and attitude set the direction of your compass in life. For an example, if you often feel sad or angry, you are operating at a lower energy frequency level. You'll attract other energy fields that will bring you more things, situations, and people that will keep you in the sad and angry spaces. However, positive emotions such as gratitude and joy operate at a higher energy frequency level. You'll attract more things that will allow you to be more grateful and bring you much joy.

Know that we are the reflection of the God, which serves as our strong foundation to claiming all of the good, abundance and treasures of this world. If we look at the word, "I AM", it has a significant meaning. An affirmation beginning with "I AM" calls the conscience mind to embrace God's presence within us. Since you and I are spiritual beings and made up of energy, it makes it easier to align with the natural energies of what surround us. We sometimes fail to attract the things we desire due to not understanding the magnitude of who we are and the power we carry being made in the reflection of God. Therefore, when your spoken word starts with "I AM", and since this is God's name stated in the bible, and then it should appropriately be followed by something powerful and of great meaning and presence.

Continue to keep in mind that we create our own reality by exercising our choice or free will and developing an understanding of how to consciously aligning our thoughts and emotions to attract specific outcomes. Now let's talk about how we can synchronize ourselves with the Universal laws and positive thinking to start creating.

CHAPTER 1:

The Universal Laws

"Attracting Abundance"

God created the universe, and the creator of all that is and part of "all that is". God is everything, pure energy, indefinite and unlimited. The universe is continually producing, and thriving in an endless cycle of abundance. The "Law of Abundance" states that there is more than enough for everyone.

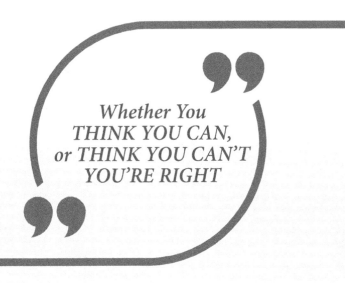

Whether You **THINK YOU CAN,** *or THINK YOU CAN'T YOU'RE RIGHT*

The universe is so abundant with resources that each of us can be completely happy and fulfilled with. There is an unlimited source of everything we need or could ever want. This great abundance is already ours, infinitely available to all of us all the time. It is always at work and always producing an abundance of something regardless if we know this or not.

We are also the infinite body of God and the extension of nature and the natural laws that are in existence. This is why one of the very best ways to know God, is through the knowing of self, "I AM". Best practice is to learn yourself, and who you are and what you can do by looking internally and creating within yourself. Belief is the seed you sowed to create an abundance of whatever you choose to believe.

Then we have the Law of Attraction, which states that what we focus on will determine what shows up in our lives. It is the ability of faith to affect physical changes in the universe. The law of Abundance and the Law of Attraction works together to bring forth the things, situations and people you tend to give more focus to whether positive or negative. Everything is energy, including us.

We are always vibrating at a particular level. We determine the quality of our thoughts, emotions, and how we choose to response or react to our experiences in life. By focusing our attention on who we are, our whole being begins to vibrate more largely. Since like attracts like, we draw to ourselves anything that is in sync with our energies. If your thoughts coupled by your emotions are continually focusing on lack, you are in essence providing the universe with the seeds to work with, which can only produce a harvest of lack and limitations in your life. However, to receive a different harvest you will need to change the underlying seeds that the Law will utilizes to produce your harvest.

You can change yourself simply by making a choice to "consciously" align and harmonize your thinking with what you desire to attract into your life. Your consciousness is your awareness of your thoughts, memories, feelings, sensations, and environment. You can experience an increase in love, joy, prosperity, gratitude, and deeper consciousness of who you are through consistent focus.

Your task is simply to clearly define the why and the what. Then, the Universe will provide the when and the how. The Universal Laws are always in action and working. The more intentional, focused, and consistent you are in doing your part, the quicker Universal Laws work. Using affirmations is a great way to plant the seeds to attracting more of what you want. When you declare and affirm something with your thoughts, emotions and actions, then the Universe brings it to you by making your affirmations become a reality.

Look at your life and your level of consciousness and quality of thoughts. If you are unfulfilled or unclear about your life's direction, then take a closer look at yourself.... your core beliefs, actions, etc. Does fear arises when you think about your dreams, goals or aspirations? Are you happy with yourself and by yourself? If you answer, "yes", you are holding to a limited belief. Meaning, there's a part of you that doesn't believe that you deserve or worthy of what you are asking for. You'll have to take a deeper look into what limited beliefs you are holding to create change.

Do you know our words strongly influence our thoughts and feelings? Do you say the phrases, "I'm just hanging in there", "I just have bad luck"? Or, if your thoughts and emotions are consistently engaging in low frequency vibrations such as fear, depression, anxiety, anger, etc., you will only attract more of the same. However, if you choose to create thoughts and emotions that engage in high frequency vibrations such as joy, happiness, gratitude, etc., you will consciously align with high frequency vibrations leading to more fulfillment and abundance in your life.

Furthermore, many of us were conditioned to believe that focusing on our needs is "selfish" and that we should always give to others before ourselves. I came to see that the only way I can give to others is when I'm tapped into my own source of wellbeing first. You can learn to rescue, "You" and not assigned this job to no one else.

Many people have the "Rescuer Syndrome", which is the need to rescue everybody else, or fix others, but themselves. I may be describing you. This behavior is often an indicator that a person is avoiding to address their own personal issues, but finds it easier to vicariously help someone else with their issues instead of working on their own problems. It's simply a way of using others as a distraction from doing the real work on them. Remember that we become empowered when we can first rescue ourselves before we can be valuable in helping others find their own way. Keep in mind that you can't help someone who doesn't want to be help.

Some of us are currently evolving and our connections to people and things are also evolving. Earlier, I mentioned how our vibration attracts the type of people we bring into our lives. Everyone has a unique energy vibration. On an energy level, if you raise your vibration and someone you know stays the same, you will begin to have less in common with that person, and won't connect like before, as both of you are evolving at different speed. I have a favorite saying that I often says, "If you change the locks, you must also change the key to unlock it, or you won't have access".

Avoid stressing out when you're no longer connecting with that person the same way. Some of you may feel guilty about your disconnections, but remember you deserve to live the highest and best version of yourself. You can lovingly love someone at a distance. When I do cross path with people I've disconnected from, I like to leave them with nuggets of reminders that they can also reach their full potential. In good scenarios, I'm able to encourage some people to start making personal changes, while others chose to remain where they are. Both way, God gave us free will and we all have a choice on how we spend our time and with whom.

You were created from greatness for greatness. You are not the norm, and you are a miracle. As a Devine creation, you are naturally a creator. There's no need to fear or be intimidate by the power to create the unseen. You are a chosen spiritual being having a human experience on earth; not the other way around. Some of us get so caught up in our human experience and forget that we are powerful spiritual being. To feel complete and whole, you must first accept the truth of its' existence.

CHAPTER 2:

Abundantly
Blessed

"You've already equipped with everything you'll need."

The first step towards getting somewhere is to decide you're not going to stay where you are. We all have needs, whether it is physical, emotional, mental and spiritual. Often, it's your own fears about the people and things in your life that can cause you so many conflicts. We search for love and validations from other people, things, and our statutes. This need for acceptance drives us to control everything and everyone around us in order to feel worthy. Yet, the only thing we are fully in control of is what's happening within us. Don't get fooled believing that we can control other people. We still need their permissions and submissions to control them. However, without their permissions we are only left with controlling own state.

No simple exercises or affirmations and visualizations are going to work, unless you remove limited thoughts and feelings. Some of us are still asking God to give us things that God already says, "Yes" to. Or, we are searching for answers that were already given, and for solutions to problems already solved. However, if we understand the capacity of who we are, it will bring us to a place of understanding that abundance is already given not be chase.

The moment you make a choice to truly see that you already have everything you need to feel happy, more than enough, and fulfilled, the faster you will become aligned with the law of abundance. Your experience of abundance is dependent on your particular alignment with it. For example, when you think about prosperity the words "thriving" and "successful" may come to mind. You must feel that you are already successful and thriving to attract more abundance.

When I started accepting my authentic self, this is when I started to realize that I already had everything I needed in order to feel genuinely whole and with a deeper sense of purpose. It feels awesome accepting my wholeness to include my strengths and weaknesses without the fear of being judged, or misunderstood by others. One of my favorite creeds I adopted in my life is written by the author and Don Miguel Ruiz, in his book, "The Four Agreements". He writes:

> *"Even the opinions you have about yourself are not necessarily true; therefore you don't need to take whatever you hear in your own mind personally…Don't take anything personally because by taking things personally you set yourself up to suffer for nothing….When we really see other people as they are without taking it personally, we can never be hurt by what they say or do. Even if others lie to you, it is okay. They are lying to you because they are afraid.*

> *There is a huge amount of freedom that comes to you when you take nothing personally. You become immune to black magicians, and no spell can affect you regardless of how strong it may be. The whole world can gossip about you, and if you don't take it personally, you are immune. Someone can intentionally send emotional poison, and if you don't*

take it personally, you will not eat it. When you don't take the emotional poison, it becomes even worse in the sender, but not in you.

As you make a habit of not taking anything personally, you won't need to place your trust in what others do or say. You will only need to trust yourself to make responsible choices. You are never responsible for the actions of others; you are only responsible for you. When you truly understand this, and refuse to take things personally, you can hardly be hurt by the careless comments or actions of others.

If you keep this agreement, you can travel around the world with your heart completely open and no one can hurt you. You can say, "I love you," without fear of being ridiculed or rejected. You can ask for what you need.

When you are convinced of the truth that "all things are working together for your highest good", your life will begin to be more like an adventure. The best way for you to experience a new reality is to reflect on how you can change the way you respond to what's happening in your life. Your new response will generate a new result, in which you'll experience a new reality. Simply think, believe, and behave that you already have everything you need to succeed and you will.

CHAPTER 3:

Understanding How to Shape Your Reality

"Reality Check."

An affirmation is often a sentence or phrase that you regularly declare to the world of what you hold to be true. Thus, when you make a statement about *"who you are"* it is more powerful than when you speak about "what you have" or "what you do". The thoughts that go through your head create who you are. Thoughts cause a reaction, and that reaction drives how you perceive your reality, the decisions you make and how you behave.

Affirmations are like seeds planted in soil. Poor soil yields poor growth and rich soil yields plentiful growth. Thus, when you make speak words to describe who you are, you are teaching the rest of the world how to receive you. In other words, you've set the tone and provide the training manual to how the world treats us. There are a few reasons using affirmations to create your reality may not work. Often, people don't know how to use affirmations correctly. Most people recite affirmations, but don't believe them. Also, when people say that "affirmations don't work", which is an affirmation in itself.

The way you choose to think, right now, is a choice. You may not realize it because you've thought this way for so long, but it really is a choice. You can choose at this very moment to change your thinking. The only moment you truly have now is this present moment. You can't guarantee what will happen tomorrow or go back to the past.

Secondly, many people tell themselves over and over what they don't want. *I' don't want to argue. "I don't want to be in debt". "I don't want to fail this class".* However, the only thing the mind can do is make a picture of the mentioned thing. Thirdly, some people will say their affirmations once a day and complain the rest of the time. If you say more negative statements than positive, which affirmation do you think will win? The negative one is the correct answer, because it's part of a long-standing, habitual way of looking at life.

The fact is that the negative programmed affirmations tend to take precedence because those are repeated so often, unintentionally and with great feelings. It will take a long time for affirmations to work if they're done that way. A working affirmation is stated in the positive. In another word, say what you do want! The more frequently you think positive and empowering thoughts that you believe in, the quicker the affirmations work.

Additionally, people often state their affirmations in the future tense like: 'I will be rich' or 'I am going to be happy'. Affirmations like 'I wish" or " I want" may not work because it does not focus on the "now". There is only "now", what's happening at this moment. So, the best way is to state your affirmation firmly in the present tense: *'I am happy'. 'I am rich.'* If you worry about *how* your affirmations will come true, you're just interrupting the whole process.

An affirmation works by creating an active vibration that needs to match what you believe and feel. When there's a delay or you don't receive what you desire, is that there's a part of you that doesn't believe that you deserve what you are asking for. The Universe can't bring you what you're asking until you release limited beliefs, thoughts and feelings about the subject. For example, if you say, "I'm smart", which is at a higher vibration, but what you're actually feeling is "I'm really not that smart", the energy force you're producing, is contrasting. This will create a tense feeling within that will serve as a blockage, then you're your affirmation will not be effective.

If the truth is that you don't feel smart, you can still change things on your end by becoming more aligned with what you really want to feel. You can do so by raising your standards and the quality of your thoughts. Start by finding things about yourself that you like and identifying areas in your life that you feel you are proud of, fulfilled and brings you joy. Also, do think about what you are grateful for to increase her energy level to manifest more quickly.

Lastly, In order for the affirmation to work your mind has to be able to accept it, believe it, and this requires a reference point. For example: saying an affirmation like "I'm a millionaire" maybe difficult to accept unless you were once a millionaire. You can't go from poverty to riches without a change in consciousness. The misconception is being rich is about having money, or whatever else you lack. However, the truth is you must be rich in consciousness before you can have riches in money or anything else in abundance.

You can use affirmations that help with your mental shift. For example, increase of income affirmations can state: *There are plenty of ways to set up multiple streams of income to make a million dollars, or "I've found the right way to make a million dollars", can be easier to accept because the mind and subconscious mind can begin to accept the possibility, and you can come up with many ways that people have made a million dollars.* Your affirmations should be believable and support the affirmation by giving it examples of how they can be achieved.

Take a good look at what you are doing or not doing that is interrupting the manifestation process for yourself. Your life won't turn around overnight, but if you're consistent and make a choice on a daily basis to think thoughts that make you feel good, you'll definitely make positive changes in every area of your life. Affirmations by themselves won't manifest anything unless you focus on what you're saying, you believe in it, and you act accordingly. Trust yourself and the process to bring your goals to life.

CHAPTER 4:

Affirmations Life Class

"Tips to Affirming What You Want"

Positive affirmations are a fantastic simple tool for focusing your thoughts on a positive change you want to manifest. Increase your chances of having effective affirmations and maximize your efforts by knowing the guidelines to the good practice of affirmations.

Here Are Nine (9) Ways to Make Your Affirmations More Effective & Powerful.

1. *Determine what your transformation looks like.* By having a picture, it brings clarity and allows you to know when you achieve it. What's the perfect life looks like for you? What quality, attitude, or value, you want to develop in yourself. Who do you want to surround yourself with? Where do you see yourself, or want to go? What goals are you targeting?

2. *Prep your atmosphere.* Picture your surroundings and what you are trying to create in your life. Evaluate where you are and identified what's stopping you from receiving what you desire. Make a list of your negative qualities, including any criticisms that you've been holding onto. Remember, we are imperfect as human beings. Sometimes, negative thoughts are hard to catch, but they have a pattern. Usually, it can start with "I can't", " I don't", and illicit negative emotions

such as anger, sadness, fear, etc. Simply make a note of them and look for a common pattern, such as "mistrust" or "unworthiness". This will be a great place to start making changes.Positive feelings are at a higher vibration and frequency. While negative feelings exist at a low vibration. A person with a higher vibration will create their desires easier, faster and more effectively than someone who is experiencing a lower vibration will show up.

3. *Write out your positive affirmations.* Began to create affirmations that challenge your limited beliefs. Write positive statements about yourself and your life. Find words that are powerful and empowering that builds you up. You may feel huge resistance as you do it. Maybe you won't believe a thing you write. No worries! Don't force yourself to believe them, just say them. Repeat them over and over again, and the affirmation will naturally become more comfortable for you to say and believe.

4. *State your affirmations in the present.* Refrain from using timebased words that refer to the future. Phrases such as "I will", "In the future", 'Tomorrow'" etc. The reason is that our brains do not always follow the concept of time. Write and say your affirmation as though you are experiencing what you desire right now.

Use your affirmations to create an inner experience is at this very moment. Example: *I'm giving and receiving loving actions in my relationship.*

5. Speak the affirmation out loud repeatedly and actively visualize your affirmations. Repeatedly say your affirmations. As you repeat your affirmations, vividly visualize yourself experiencing them. Make a conscious effort to deeply feel them. This is very powerful because it engages your senses and will help with rewiring your mind to move from the concept of the affirmation to real life. Also, it's desirable that you use affirmations in a relaxed state of mind, so that your mind can receive everything you give to it. You can carry your written affirmations with you. If you need a pick-me-up, or if you find yourself about steering away from your goals, get out your affirmations out and read them.

"There were several things I desired and was able to manifest in my life. I think about what I desired often with great feelings and visualized as if I already have them over and over. In due time, they will showed up."

6. *Engage in meditation.* You can repeat it silently to yourself as you breathe and let this repetition be a space for your mind to rest while you meditate. We an plant our affirmation seeds in the subconscious mind.

With continued practice, this thought-picture grows in strength and become a new habit leading to a new way of living and manifesting our desires.

7. *Stay consistent* – Repetition and consistency are the keys if you want to create changes using affirmations. Make a commitment to recite your affirmations daily. Saying your affirmations once a day will have little impact. You need to say your affirmations regularly throughout the day. For example: If you want to get a new job and you say I've found a new job, you can't follow it up with a series of negative thoughts like *"Nobody is hiring", "It's hard to get hired",* etc. For the affirmation to work, you have to have an attitude and thought the process that is aligned with what you want to achieve. Some ways to keep consistent is to keep a journal writing your affirmations daily, meditate on your affirmations and post your affirmation in areas of eye view to keep them relevant to you.

8. *Be faithful.* Affirmations are more effective when practiced with faith and belief. Doubt and insecurity undermine your positive affirmations, which will work against you. For maximum benefit, carry out your affirmation with faith, trust, and belief you already have it.

9. *Say "Yes" when opportunities show up.* Sometimes we will ask for things, but when the opportunity shows up we failed to take advantage of it. Sometimes, what we asked for shows up in not the best timing, or how we pictured it, etc. When that happens, many people tend to find many excuses as to why they can't say, "Yes". This form of behavior can be very subtle and hard to catch. So, pay close attention to how you respond to opportunities when they appear during unexpected or unfavorable conditions. Below, I'll describe a past experience with learning to say, "Yes".

When it shows up, be ready to receive it.

In this past year, I thought about traveling more and experiencing new places. I didn't have a specific place I wanted to travel to. However, I did have pictures of various places I would like to travel to and pictures of travel bags, and airplanes on my vision board (created several months prior). I would visualize traveling to different parts of the world from cruising on the waters in the Caribbean to site seeing in Europe. Also, I would recite various affirmations to support my travel vision, which consist of, "I'm travelling around the world"; "I'm enjoying my exotic trips".

A couple of months later, I was invited to travel to the island of Aruba in the Caribbean with a group of friends. My first reaction is to say "Yes". However, there was a " but " that followed after. I had a few reservations about going on this trip. It was short notice. I needed to rearrange my work schedule, and budget my traveling expenses.

The opportunity to travel didn't look like how I envisioned. I imagine having enough time to plan a trip ahead of time to workout the logistics. Not necessarily a spur in the moment opportunity. It suddenly dawn on me that I was blocking my desires to travel from manifesting. I also thought to myself, "What other areas in my life am I blocking because the opportunity present itself differently than what I expected"? At that point, I made the decision to go on the trip. I started to focus on the "how I can make it happen", instead of "why it can't happen".

Since I became more intentional with my thoughts and actions, I found my way to Aruba and had a blast. Moving forward, I became more deliberate with saying, 'Yes" when opportunities show up, even if I don't know the "how". I just figure it out later. Needless to say, in the same year, I traveled to five other places domestically and overseas because I was intentional with manifesting my desire to travel. I share this story with you, so I can bring it to your attention to be intentional with creating the experiences you desire in life.

Now I ask you, what things are you blocking from manifesting? What things have you ask for, but you've talked yourself out of doing? Maybe you say things like, "It's not the right time". Or, "I don't have enough money to do it", "I don't know how to do it". When all you'll need is to put yourself in the mindset of already having what you want, speaking as if you already received it. You'll began finding what you'll need to complete your goal. When you are in alignment with what you want, the universe will figure out the most efficient and harmonious way to bring it to you. It may not show up how you envisioned it, but when it does shows up, be open to receive it.

Now, are you blocking the things you ask for from manifesting? What things have you ask for that you've talked yourself or out of doing? Maybe you say things like, "It's not the right time". Or, "I don't have enough money to do it", "I don't know how to do it". When all you'll need is to put yourself in the mindset of already having what you want, stating it as if you already received it, and finding how you can attract what you need to complete the goal. When you are in alignment with what you want, the universe will figure out the most efficient and harmonious way to bring it to you. It may not show up how you envisioned it, but when it does shows up, say, "Yes".

CHAPTER 5:

Receptive Giver

"Willingly Giving"

We've all heard the words "It's better to give than receive. To start receiving, we must first give. It is up to us to initiate the giving and receiving cycle. You always have something to give; time, compliments, smiles, talent, money, knowledge, share a book, etc. Whatever energy you give will come back to you. It is the energy behind the giving that matters, so do not give grudgingly.

Often because of our societal conditioning, we believe that in order to be a "good" person, we must give. Accepting this as truth, force us to "give" in situations where we really don't want to. This is never a good idea. The intention behind our giving and receiving is the most important thing. When the act of giving is joyful, when it is unconditional, and from the heart, then the energy behind the giving increases many times over. However, if we give grudgingly, the wrong energy behind that giving will not cause increase.

The Law of Giving and Receiving is simple. If you want love, learn to give love; if you want attention, learn to give attention; if you want to be blessed with all the good things in life, learn to bless others with the good things in life. The more you give, the more you will receive. In your willingness to give that which you seek, you will keep the abundance of the universe circulating in your life.

The best way to experience the Law of Giving and Receiving is to give a gift to everyone you come into contact with. This doesn't have to be in the form of material things. The gifts of affection, time, prayers, and words or encouragement are some of the great gifts you can give, and they don't cost you anything. Give wherever you go, and as you give, you will receive. As you receive, the more your ability to give will increase, and the more you'll benefit.

When we are connected with our own source energy, we can't help but give. It flows into you and out in all directions. From that place, you will give truly and automatically from the heart, and the quality of your giving will touch everyone you meet, even if you never even say a word or "do" anything.

CHAPTER 6:

Learning How to Receive

"Comfortably Accepting"

Everything in the universe operates through active mutual exchange. Giving and receiving are the infinity symbol of reciprocation. Both are vital to the larger whole. Every relationship is one of give and take, because giving and receiving are different aspects of the flow of energy in the universe. Success is connected to the flow of giving and receiving. Therefore, the only way to create abundance in life is by regulating the dynamics of giving and receiving at both, the conscious and subconscious levels. When we attain balance, we create abundance and prosperity in our lives and the lives of those around us.

If we look at receiving, most of us were never taught how to receive. The ironic thing is that receiving is actually an innate "skill" that we all have. Our society conditions us to seize what we want and often we don't know how to receive what is already abundantly given to us by our creator. Consequently, we need to practice something that is already as natural to us as breathing. Social conditioning has a habit of making us feel wary about openly accepting compliments, generosity, and other kind acts, or, we'll be seen as greedy, or selfish.

Also, receiving involves vulnerability, while giving makes you feel in charge. When you receive, you feel less in charge. It may be difficult for some to just receive. When you receive, you'll be in harmony with the law of giving and receiving. It is important first, to become more aware of your personal dynamic for receiving or not receiving. Allowing yourself to receive will awaken your own natural state, and you'll be able to observe the Law of Abundance in action. You'll understand how it feels to receive more than you could ever imagine. You will also feel profound gratitude that someone wants to be of service to you.

The Law of Abundance is about our ability to open up and be aware of the flow of high frequency emotions like love, gratitude, and joy that is always flowing and available to us. What we desire may appear as a byproduct. The abundance we're speaking of is the experience of being tapped into Source Energy, which determines the quality of our lives. Out of that, all good things flow to us, both physical objects and non physical experiences that nourish and affirm our hearts. However! It is never too late to learn to be open and experience abundance.

To learn how to receive, simply open your heart, live in the moment and cherish the fact that other people care so deeply about you that you are connected, needed, and wanted. When we've discovered and opened up the channel of abundance within us, we consciously give attention to this flow, and then we will vibrate in harmony with abundance and therefore manifest it in our physical lives. Below are tips you can use to practice receiving.

To Experience the Law of Giving and Receiving:

• Give a gift of compliment, a card, or a prayer to those you encounter. This will begin the process of circulating joy and affluence in your life and the lives of others.

• Be gratefully when you receive every gift that comes your way, no matter the size.

• Focus on the positive nurturing positive energy and expanding it in your life. You'll attract more positive experiences to come your way.

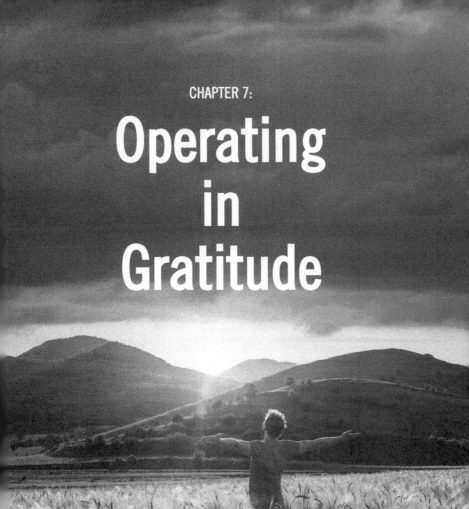

CHAPTER 7:

Operating
in
Gratitude

"The Grateful Being"

When was the last time you stopped to really acknowledge the things you're thankful for? Gratitude is an emotion expressing appreciation for what one has. One of the quickest ways to be aligned with The Law of Abundance is to think about what you are grateful for. Some of us appear to never to be satisfied with what we have rich or poor, healthy or sick. It will make a huge difference, when we realize that everything we have has been given to us by God.

Gratitude gets you attracting more good things into your life quickly. Practicing gratitude will tend to give you a widened perspective. You may have lost someone, your job recently; or, you may have a disability or illness that makes life difficult. However, being a the state of gratitude will allow you to handle those frustrations with more wisdom, because you'll see the big picture, and acknowledge it could be worse or there are other people going to worst situation.

People who are thankful for the things in their lives aren't living an easier life than you, but they understand that the situation isn't the problem, but how they think about the situation that makes the difference. The benefits of practicing gratitude are continuous. People who regularly practice gratitude experience more positive emotions, have better health, sleep better, express more compassion and kindness.

Our relationships with others plays an important role in shaping our happiness since we spend a huge amount of time with people whether is our family, in our jobs, schools, etc. Gratitude strengthens relationships and makes us feel closer and more committed to our relatives, friends and romantic partners. In conclusion, the simple acts of gratitude don't cost you much to do, but will cost you if you don't do it.

CHAPTER 8:

Activities to Attract More of What You Want

In this chapter, I'm going to share with you cool activities that you can use as tools to support you in your quest of manifesting your dream life.

Activity 1: Vision Boarding
A vision board, also known as a goal board, or a goal map that serves as a powerful visualization tool. It connects to the Law of Attraction to motivate you to take the steps needed to accomplish your intentions, dreams, goals, and vision. A vision board uses visual descriptions or is a collage of the goals and things that you want to have, be, or do in your life. Consider it as your affirmations being illustrated on a board. Vision boards will help you identify your vision and give it clarity and reinforce your daily affirmations.

It consists of a poster or foam board with cut out pictures, drawings and or writing of the things that you want in your life glued on the board. The purpose of a vision board is to activate the law of attraction to begin to attracting things, situations, etc. from your surroundings to begin to the manifestation process. You can start by selecting pictures and writing that you have a connection or illicit strong emotions to increase motivation.

Creating your vision board
Your personal vision board is based on the level of your creativity. I've outlined below guidelines to creating a purposeful vision board that can be used by anyone.

The elements of a well-designed vision board should include:

Pro Visual: Make your vision board as visual as possible. The idea behind this is that when you surround yourself with images of who you want to become it helps you to reach your objectives by providing emphasis to whatever is being said. Your pictures and words should be used to reinforce your message, goals, clarify points, and create excitement.

Make it detailed: It's important to be specific with your goals when posting what you would like to manifest. When you set specific goals, they become real and more attainable. Instead of saying "I want a better life" or "I want to be rich," say "I have a job doing X, making X per month" or "I' travel to X." Post pictures that represent your goals.

Emotional Connectedness: Each picture on your vision board should stir up a positive emotional response from you. When you look at your vision board, you should be inspired, motivated and eager to achieve what you place on there every time you look at it. Additionally, you might want to add writing or drawing on your vision board you better resonate with.

Intentional positioning: You'll need to constantly expose your subconscious mind to your board in order to manifest your desires quicker. Place your vision board in eyesight and in a location that gives you maximum exposure to it. The common places are in your bedroom, at your office desk, etc. I created replicas of my actual vision board and save it to the screens on my phone and computer.

Update your vision board. When you achieve a visual goal on your board, scratch it off and replace it with a new goal. Also, you might find that some of the images on your vision board don't really carry as much emotional impact on you as they did before. When this happens, you'll want to update your vision board with new fresh images that do inspire you.

In conclusion, vision boards are an important tool in your success tool box. They are cheap to create. They are also a great way of keeping your attention on your intentions. Are you ready to get started on your vision board? If, you already have one, does it need an update?

Activity 2: The Memo
This activity is a beautiful reminder that you have the capacity to do whatever you want with your life right now. Sometimes, you may need to hear an encouraging message to motivate you to keep it going. This activity is for you to find creative ways to send personal messages to yourself to give you continuous reminders of encouragements. It can include you recording a message to yourself containing your affirmations that you can replay at any time. Or, if you have a space where you can write your affirmations throughout your room such as a chalkboard, notepad, post them on the walls, or write empowering phrases

on your mirror with erasable markers, etc. This will help you stay focus and aligned to what you would like to achieve. Come up with a way for you can train your subconscious to adapt to the message you want to believe.

Activity 3: The Power of Visualization
Visualization is an integral part of the manifesting process. We use it to focus the creative power within us to attract the things we desire. A successful visualization can make our brain believe that what we're desire is actually happening. When we visualize, we do it always in the present tense, as if has already happened or is happening now. We use all of our senses to enhance the feeling that what we're visualizing is real.

Use your affirmation to help with a shift in perspective shift if it's challenging to see request what you want. For example, if you just ended a relationship and know you're not ready for another relationship at this moment. Instead of saying I'm in a new relationship and not really feel it. You can say, "I'm open to being in a healthy relationship. Then visualize that you're opening to being in a relationship and all that you have let go of all of your reservations and limitations about relationships and purely enjoy the freedom and excitement of being in a healthy relationship. Be open to receiving, without any negative emotion, like fear or doubt.

Activity 4: The Focus Wheel

The Focus Wheel Process was presented by Abraham-Hicks, an inspirational speaker. A focus wheel is to shift your focus onto more positive thoughts and attitudes when it comes to the things you want to attract. According to the Law of Attraction, how you feel about a topic is your point of attraction. For example, if you dislike your job or not having a job, you most likely feel "frustrated" about the path of you are on. With the Law of Attraction, you will draw in more frustrations, disappointments, or other emotions similar in frequency. Creating a focus wheel will redirect your vibration and give you a different outcome.

To start, first identify what you don't want. For example, you might think to yourself: I don't want to feel disappointed about my job, relationships, etc. I don't want to feel fearful with starting a business, or making a commitment to someone, etc. Having decided what you don't want, you can now easily identify what you do want. Now affirm what you want by writing it in an affirmation.

Examples:
• I have satisfying and fulfilling relationships in my life.
• I'm working my dream job that enhances my skills.

Directions:

Grab a piece of paper, draw a circle in the center, and write what you want. For example: to be healthy, financial freedom, a loving partner, owning your business, etc. Next, write down a positive belief you have about the subject, placing this belief around the edge of the central circle. So someone hoping for a better relationship might say: "I do enjoy meeting new people".

For example, referencing the goal of starting a new business, you might write the positive belief "I have a great education in how to plan a business."Keep going, writing as many positive beliefs as you can find, always around the circle. If this statement is true and matches what's in the center of the wheel and it makes you feel better, even slightly, write it down on the first position of the wheel.

If the statement doesn't make you feel good, keep looking. Eventually, your page will be full of statements that support your belief in the reality you want to manifest. If you like, add this focus wheel to your dream board, or just pin it to your fridge or front door to keep you connected with its truth.

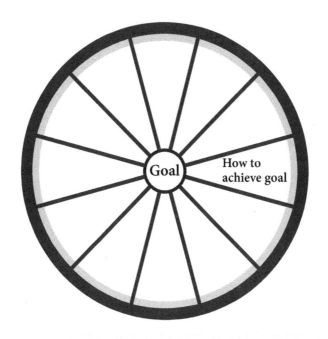

Focus Wheel Example. Figure 1

Activity 5: The Law of Abundance Check

Here is a fun way to use the Law of Abundance. Take a blank check from your check book. Date it for that day, address it to yourself, and put in an amount that you'd like to receive, and then sign it "Law of Abundance." Put the check in your purse, wallet or pocket. You can use this on your vision board, paste it in a place that you will see it regularly or keep it with you. Look at it as often and feel how it feels to receive the amount from The Law of Abundance. Also be open minded so you can actually see the gifts that are presented to you. It can come in other forms of opportunities that can be the stepping stone to more. For example, a series of small gifts, or a larger gift.

CHAPTER 9:

Affirmations Boot Camp Segment #1: A's

In order to help you get started in creating and manifesting the goals and experiences you desire, in these next chapters, you will be receive several affirmations you can apply to various areas of your life.

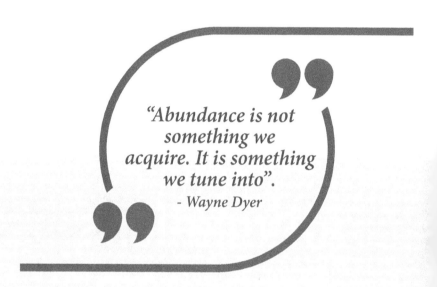

"Abundance is not something we acquire. It is something we tune into".
- *Wayne Dyer*

Abundance

"I AM Created Out of Abundance to Live Abundantly"

Abundance is an extremely plentiful or overflowing quantity or supply; affluence; wealth, etc.

The secret to the law of abundance is to focus on what you desire with positive emotion and enthusiasm. Sometimes it can seem difficult to focus on being positive if we are experiencing stream of problems like losing someone, not enough money to pay the bills, people letting us down, and any number of these things occurring can seem to hinder our way and block us from seeing the greatness of our days. If your thoughts are consistently focused on lack and limitations, the Law of Abundance will provide you with an abundance of lack and limitations in your life.

Regardless if you choose to do so consciously, or unconsciously, you'll receive an abundance of that something, whether you like what you receiving or not. However, you have to practice seeing beyond your circumstances and challenges and to remaining hopeful that it will change for the better. Our current limitations do not represent the abundance of blessings that awaits us. Remember that there is no limit to what the universe can offer to you. And if you focus on lack and scarcity, then you will also be able to experience this as well.

One great way to keep your thoughts focus on what you want is to use abundance affirmations. Affirming what you want more of will only help the process of delivery. Living in an abundance state is living with no doubt, not carrying negative emotions and being in a state of gratitude.

You are a blessed human being whether you know it. You were created to live abundantly and without worries. However, we forgot who we are and our purpose, which often lead to our ability to be in the state of abundance.

Here are a few affirmations that can help you embrace the law of abundance:

- The universe is an abundant place that has more than enough for me to achieve everything I desire.
- I have what I need, and more of what I want is coming.
- I am an abundant person in mind, body and spirit.
- I am so grateful now that I am enough & have enough.
- I am whole and thriving.
- I'm a reflection of the creator, an unlimited spiritual being.
- I'm grateful for all I am and what life is here to teach me.

Addiction

"I Conquer All Things That Are Not Part of My Natural Fabric"

Addiction is a condition that results when a person ingests a substance (e.g., alcohol, cocaine, nicotine, prescription) or engages in an activity (e.g., gambling, sex, shopping) that can be pleasurable but the continued use or act of which becomes compulsive and interferes with ordinary life responsibilities, such as work, relationships, or health. Also, a

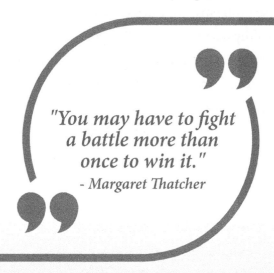

"You may have to fight a battle more than once to win it."
- Margaret Thatcher

Many of us can use substances or become engaged in activities without any significant problems. Some people, however, may experience damaging psychological and/or physical effects when their habit becomes an addiction. Addictions are generally caused by a combination of physical, mental, circumstantial and emotional factors. Most experts agree that addiction is a brain disease, but that doesn't mean you're a helpless victim. The brain changes associated with addiction can be treated and reversed through therapy, and other treatments. If the drug fulfils a valuable need or fills a void, you may find yourself increasingly relying on it. What began as a voluntary choice has turned into a physical and psychological need.

For example, you may take drugs to calm you if you feel stressed, or make you more confident in social situations.

Until you find alternative, healthier methods for overcoming these problems, your drug use will likely continue. To maintain healthy balance in your life, you need to have other positive experiences, to feel good in your life aside from any drug use. Recovery from drug addiction is a long process that often involves setbacks. Relapse doesn't mean that treatment has failed or that you're a lost cause. Rather, it's a signal to get back on track, either by going back to treatment or adjusting the treatment approach.

Affirmations to help you with addiction:
- I am free from my addiction (drug, sex, etc.)
- I am responsible for my thoughts, beliefs, and actions.
- I respect and love my body, and accept myself fully, completely, and unconditionally.
- I'm valuable, and my mistakes don't define me.
- I forgive myself and those I've hurt.
- I take accountability for my treatment.

Anxiety

"I AM built To Overcome"

Anxiety is an emotion characterized by an unpleasant state of inner turmoil, often accompanied by nervous behavior, such as pacing back and forth, somatic complaints and rumination.

"Nothing in the affairs of men is worthy of great anxiety."
- Plato

Anxiety is a normal human emotion that everyone experiences at times. Many people feel anxious, or nervous, when faced with a problem in life, or making an important decision. Anxiety, worry, and stress are all a part of most people's life today. In fact, anxiety is a necessary warning signal of a dangerous or difficult situation. Without anxiety, we would have no way of anticipating difficulties ahead and preparing for them. However, if not controlled anxiety become a problem and can negatively interfere with our functioning in life.

If you have experienced an anxiety attack, you may be fearful of having another one, but living in such fear means you are living in a state of perpetual anxiety. This can happen just because you are afraid of the anxiety itself! The subconscious mind holds our beliefs which in turn guide our life, if we can reprogram the subconscious mind, it should become easier to control or even cure the anxiety problem. Controlling how you view stressful situations will help you stay focus on living life more efficiently.

Using anxiety affirmations can help you overcome fear and help you begin to live your life again.

- I am cool, calm and collected in any situation.
- I overcome my fear of anything and everything and live life courageously.
- Every cell in my body is relaxed and oozes out calmness.
- I replace indecision with focused decisive action.
- I rise above stress of any kind. I live in peace.

CHAPTER 10:

Affirmations Boot Camp Segment #2: C's

Career

"I AM Driven To Succeed"

A career is an individual's journey through learning, work and other aspects of life.

> *"Find out what you like doing best, and get someone to pay you for it."*
> Katharine Whitehorn

We spend many of our waking hours at work, so we better love what we do. Even if you're trapped in a position you don't love, with no realistic opportunity for change, there are still ways to find more joy and satisfaction in what you do. Your attitude makes a difference. Renew, restore, and reassess where you are and where you want to go with your career goals, as well as goals in other areas of your life. Identify and honor your strengths and find out how to maximize them without being apologetic or feeling sorry. Choose to focus on the positive aspects of the job that you do enjoy even if it's just chatting with your coworkers at lunch, helping a customer solve a problem or your coworker or staff. Changing your attitude towards your job can help you regain a sense of purpose and control.

If you are looking to change directions, understand that career change doesn't often happen overnight, and it is easy to get overwhelmed with all the steps to successfully change careers. Break down large goals into smaller ones, and try to accomplish at least one small thing a day to keep the momentum going. Lastly, take care of yourself. You might be feeling so busy with the career transition that you barely have time to sleep or eat. However, managing stress, eating right, and taking time for sleep, exercise, and loved ones will ensure you have the stamina for the big changes ahead.

Soar high with using these career affirmations.

• My phone is ringing off the hook and clients lining up for miles.

• I am an expert in my field, and I receive the perfect pay and rewards for my expertise.

• I am attracting excellent job prospects all the time.

• I earn $X per month doing things that I enjoy doing.

• I love my career and my contribution to the world.

• I'm prospering everywhere I go

Courage

"I AM courageous! Just Look What I've Been Through"

Courage is the quality of mind, or spirit that enables a person to face difficulty, danger, pain, etc. The ability to act rightly in the face of popular opposition, shame, scandal or discouragement.

"A hero is one who knows how to hang on one minute"
- *Norwegian proverb*

Courage is not the absence of fear, but the strength to overcome it. Courage is not only that we face our challenges, but it is also the approach we take. Courage is being able to stand up for what you believe in and not allowing others bring you down because you are different or see things differently. Courage, like everything starts in your mind. This is a good thing because it means that who you are now and you can change and develop yourself to become courageous, fearless, and daring.

Where have you demonstrated courage in your life? Where could you use a little courage at this moment? Look closely at times you show courage. Take note that courage can be seen in different outlooks to include being able to stand firm on a decision while the majority speak out against injustice at great personal risk, the ability to take financial risks to follow your dreams to become an Entrepreneurs or walking away from a secure job, or overcoming an abusive history and still you rise, not as victim, but a survivor. You are a great person, who can do great things no matter what others think. Believe in yourself become someone who is not afraid to face their fears and can stand up and take action when needed.

Here are our positive courage affirmations. They will help you get started on the road to developing courage.

• It's okay to have opinions and to voice them.

• I am unstoppable and live courageously.

• I have the courage to show more of who I truly am.

• I breathe in my courage. I exhale my fear.

• My bold life awaits me. I answer the call.

• I act in spite of my fear, and the fear fades away.

• I boldly take every step with courage and intent.

CHAPTER 11:

Affirmations Boot Camp Segment #3: D's

Depression

"I AM Manifestation of the Divine and Will Stand As Such"

An illness that involves the body, mood, and thoughts and that affects the way a person eats, sleeps, feels about himself or herself, and thinks about things.

> "You largely constructed your depression. It wasn't given to you. Therefore, you can deconstruct it".
> - Albert Ellis

The normal ups and downs of life mean that everyone feels sad or has "the blues" from time to time. Feeling depressed can be a normal reaction to loss, life's struggles, or an injured self-esteem, but when feelings of intense sadness including feeling helpless, hopeless, worthless, and despair have taken hold of your life and won't go away for many days to weeks and keep you from functioning normally, your depression may be something more than sadness. When the feelings interfere with daily activities such as taking care of family, spending time with friends, or going to work or school, it's likely a major depressive episode.

Depression varies from person to person, and is caused by a combination of genetic, biological, environmental, and psychological factors. Depression makes it tough to function and enjoy life like you once did. Just getting through the day can be overwhelming. But no matter how hopeless you feel, you can get treated. When your symptoms are overwhelming and disabling, that's when it's time to seek professional help. If you or someone you know is depressed, contact a therapist or medical professional. The most important thing you can do is help your friend or relative get professional treatment. You may need to make an appointment and go with him or her to see the doctor.

Start conquering your depression using these affirmations:

- I courageously protect my happiness because my mind is strong.
- I wisely let go of any judgments of myself or others, easily and effortlessly.
- My thoughts are filled with positivity, and my life is plentiful with prosperity.
- I am a big gift to this world to feel, and the world is a better place because I am here.
- My worth was determined the day I was created, and it's not base on my situations, who I know or how I perform.

CHAPTER 12:

Affirmations Boot Camp Segment #4: F's

Faith

"I believe Without A Shadow of A Doubt"

Believing in something or trusting someone, especially with strong conviction; belief in the existence of God: strong religious feelings or beliefs.

"Faith is taking the first step even when you don't see the whole staircase".
- Martin Luther King, Jr.

The word faith comes from a Latin word fidere, which means to trust, believe, or have faith. Faith generally means having a strong conviction, deep trust, reliance upon, or loyalty to something. When we demonstrate faith, we're relying on something. When you sit in a chair, you're relying on the chair's manufacturer to produce something that will hold you up.

When you're on the freeway, you're relying on every other driver around you. Your faith can also refer to a religion or system of beliefs. Today we are tempted to put our faith in many things. Faith is not a thought-out set of ideas, but instead a set of impressions that are largely gained from their parents or other significant adults in their lives.

Some people trust in God, others in money, friends, self, political leaders, or military power. Still others trust in science, other experts, astrology, or fortune- tellers. Faith is a feeling and vibration. When you really have faith about something, you must feel it. It allows you to have the openness and sensitivity, not to mention imagination to make room in your heart for a larger worldview. You also will have the greater spirit to conceive of something wondrous that exists beyond the visible. This measure of faith can be increased. But you're the one who increases it.

Use these affirmations to help strengthen your faith:

• I am with God and God is with me.
• My faith in God sets me free from all worry, anxiety and doubt.
• Everything that is happening is only for the highest good of me.
• Higher spirit guides me in the direction of my dreams.
• My mind and body are in complete alignment with the Universe and I am always in the flow.
• I let go of fear, worry, and pain. I choose to live in love and peace
• My faith lifts me above my doubts.

Fear

"I AM Fearless. No Weapons Forms
Against Me Shall Prosper"

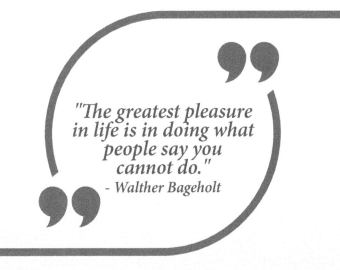

"The greatest pleasure in life is in doing what people say you cannot do."
- Walther Bageholt

Is an emotion induced by a real or imaginary threat perceived by living entities, which causes a change in brain and organ function and ultimately a change in behavior, such as running away, hiding or freezing from traumatic events.

Have you ever been so afraid of something in life? Fear is an adaptive behavior that we have to help identify threats. It is an ability that has allowed us as humans to survive predators and natural disasters. However, many of our fears are imaginary, which cause you to be immobilized. You'll end up doing nothing, stopping your forward progress in life; you're likely to miss some great opportunities along the way.

Before you can begin overcoming fear, you have to know that they are causing your fears. Get specific about what exactly you're afraid of. Look at the pictures you have in your head about the situation. When we know where they really come from, we can start to control them. Take action taker and know that fears are just fears. When you take action and face your fears, they become weaker, because you realize that reality isn't nearly as bad as your imagination. Stay positive. You really can't fail when you're always seeking the positive outcome, even though the voice inside your head tells you otherwise. Learn turning that voice off and just go for it! Getting through fear is a skill that anyone can learn. If you're at one of these crossroads in your life, let me encourage you to go forward. Remember, fear torments, and God wants to deliver you from all of your fears.

Below are a few affirmations on how to overcome fear in order to enjoy true success in life.

- I now choose love and peace instead of fear.
- Releasing all fear, I step into my purpose of accomplishing my dreams.
- My faith lifts me above all fears.
- I relinquish fear, and I get back in control.
- I live in the feelings of love, joy and abundance.
- I walk by faith

Financial Abundance

"I AM Financially Free"

Financial abundance is an extremely plentiful quantity or supply referencing financial means.

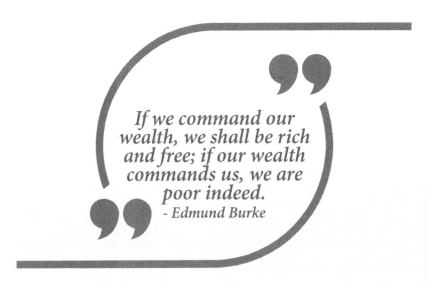

If we command our wealth, we shall be rich and free; if our wealth commands us, we are poor indeed.
- Edmund Burke

Wealth always begins with your thoughts. Wealthy thoughts create action and action leads to prosperity. If your finance is not where you want it to be then, there's a part of you that doesn't believe that you deserve what you are asking. For example, if you're declaring: "I don't have enough money," "Money is hard to come by," then perhaps you have old, deepseated beliefs that you don't deserve to prosper or you are holding on to other limited belief in your own consciousness about money. Limited beliefs about money may come from your family's belief that there's a part of you that still accepts those beliefs and continue to operate under them for the rest of our lives until we choose to really look at those beliefs and evaluate them.

If you believe money is constantly striving to get you, it will. We must be willing to become aware of where we focus our attention and what we believe to be true. The Universe can't bring you more income until you release limited beliefs, thoughts and feelings about money. The same will go for other things you're desire. Take a good look at what are you doing or not doing that are interrupting the manifestation process for yourself and pay attention to patterns you've developed.

One of the first important steps to manifest financial abundance is to be consistent and firm about improving your thoughts about money. If you instead keep focusing on things that worry you about money, or the many things you wish you could manifest but can't seem to make progress on, you'll just keep creating more of the same lacking state in your life.

Another important step is to start mending your relationship with money. How would you describe your relationship with money? Do you two have a loving relationship or an unstable one? Does money make you feel unworthy and alone frequently? Or, does money feel appreciated and loved by you? Whatever you think, feel, and expect from money, it's going to fulfill your request. Now, if money were a person, would it want to hang out with you? Think about how you treat your money. Will you be worrisome not knowing when money is coming, jealous not wanting share or keeping it all to yourself, impulsive not spending it constructively or unavailable not paying attention to money. If that were the case, money as a person would go out of its way to avoid you like a plague. It will mirror in the same manner you approach it.

Your outer world is merely a reflection of your inner relationship with everything in the world. You have to believe money is everywhere and in abundance and show all money big or small gratitude when present. Do your best to start healing your relationship with money, and you'll notice that money will respond to your efforts in abundant ways!

Also, if you often feel stressed, anxious, fearful, worried, or defeated in life in general and not just about money, but other areas of your life it may be blocking financial abundance from coming into your life. Feeling joyous, free, inspired, blessed, abundant or any other positive state, you will attract abundance.

Being in a positive state means being opened, trusting, believing and knowing that you are already abundant. Abundance just flows to you consistently and easily. You never have to strain or struggle for it. It just flows! Every day, be attentive in focusing your thoughts on the positive aspects of money and abundance. Let's also remember that it is up to each one of us to decide how to use that money as well as what meaning we give to it. We participate in the movement of positive energy and the creation of the "giving and receiving" cycle. The result is that we all flourish together.

Here are affirmations to get you started
• I am receiving infinite, inexhaustible and immediate abundance
• I am financially free and have X amount a month in passive income in my business.
• I have a healthy relationship with money.
• I embrace positive new beliefs about prosperity.
• Everyone and everything are bringing divine abundance, prosperity and love in my life.
• I am surrounded by people who are eager to contribute to my abundance each and every day.
• I 'm able to be financial blessings to others.

Forgiveness

"I AM Forgiven and Will Return the Favor"

Forgiveness is the intentional and voluntary process by which a victim undergoes a change in feelings and attitude regarding an offense; let's go of negative emotions such as vengefulness, with an increased ability to wish
the offender well.

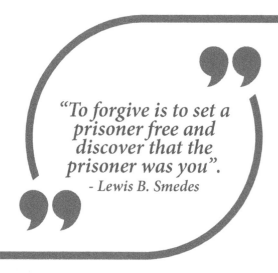

> *"To forgive is to set a prisoner free and discover that the prisoner was you".*
> *- Lewis B. Smedes*

Forgiveness can be difficult for many people simply because they are not clear about what forgiveness really is. Forgiveness is allowing yourself to be worthy of healing and to make peace from the hurtful experience and changing your grievance story. Holding on to a grudge, resentment and not forgiving that person for hurting you is agreeing to remain in bondage and be enslaved by someone else actions and deeds. You become so wrapped up in the wrong that you can't enjoy the present.

Forgiveness doesn't mean you condone a person action or agreed to what happened. It does not mean denying reality or ignoring repeated offenses or getting another person to change his or her actions, behavior or words. Some people are mean-spirited or apathetic. They never will change. We need to change the way we respond to them and quit expecting them to be different.

By forgiving, you will no longer empower the story created by someone else to continue to hurt you. As mentioned earlier, we resist forgiving because we don't really understand what forgiveness is or how it works. The first step to understanding forgiveness is giving yourself permission to forgive and letting go of the bitterness while remembering very clearly your rights to healthy boundaries.

Forgiveness is a choice we make through a decision of our will. It's also a process. It might take some time to work through our emotional problems before we can truly forgive. It's normal for memories to be triggered in the future. When thoughts of past hurts occur, it's what we do with them that count. When we find ourselves focusing on a past offense, we can learn to say, "Thank you, God, for this reminder of how important forgiveness is."

We forgive by faith, out of obedience. We must trust God to do the work in us that needs to be done so that our forgiveness will be complete. Also, the art of letting go is a skill. It is a skill that we must practice and also apply to other areas of our lives. This realization led to me think about what other things and people I've had to give up that caused me mostly pain.

Think of forgiveness more about changing your life by bringing you peace, and emotional and spiritual healing.

Forgiveness can take away the power the other person continues to have in your life. When you release the wrongdoer from the wrong, you cut a malignant tumor out of your inner life.

Affirmations for freeing yourself and forgiving:
- I ask for forgiveness from all those whom I may have wronged and forgiven all those who may have wronged me.
- I forgive everyone, especially myself, for all actions and all inactions throughout my entire life.
- I forgive myself for all my angers, resentments, and jealousies.
- I release myself from all guilt and judgment.
- I resist the temptation to judge others.
- I unconditionally forgive everyone for all hurt that I have ever experienced in the presence of their actions.
- I unconditionally forgive myself for everything that I have ever done, said, or thought that had caused me harm or suffering.

CHAPTER 13:

Affirmations Boot Camp Segment #5: G's

Gratitude

*"I AM Grateful For The Small
and Open To Receive The Bigger"*

Gratitude is a feeling or attitude in acknowledgement of a benefit that one has received or will receive.

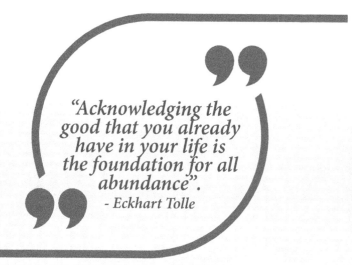

"Acknowledging the good that you already have in your life is the foundation for all abundance".
- Eckhart Tolle

The Power of Gratitude is not only an important life skill to learn and master; it's an extremely important aspect of consciously and consistently attracting more fulfillment. Developing an attitude of gratitude is one of the most important and essential things that you can do for attracting and manifesting the things that you desire into your life. Cultivating gratitude is one of the simpler routes to a greater sense of emotional well-being, higher overall life satisfaction, and a greater sense of happiness in life. It allows you to bring into your conscious awareness the good things that are happening in your life on a day to day basis, and with repetition, will take your focus off of what you perceive as the negative aspects of any situation.

Its purpose is to put you more into a mindset of finding that you really do have good, positive things happening to you in all areas of your life and shifts the focus off of what you perceive to be negative. It's hard to complain about the little things when you give thanks that you are alive and healthy. Be thankful for each new challenge, because it will build your strength and character. When you change the way you look at things, the things you look at change. One of the best ways to cultivate gratitude is to keep a gratitude journal. The benefits of journaling you are left with a nice long list of things in your life for which you are grateful. On my list, I thank my loved ones and my health. I am thankful for strangers who've shown me acts of kindness. I thank God, for the life he's given me. Think about what are you thankful for at this very moment.

Below are a few gratitude Affirmations to get you started.
- I choose to live a life of gratitude and joy, inspiring others to follow my example.
- I give thanks for the bounties of this world.
- I have gratitude for everything that has ever occurred to bring me to this moment.

- I accept the entirety of my past and my present life gratefully.
- I give thanks for everything that has occurred to bring me to this moment.

CHAPTER 14:

Affirmations Boot Camp Segment #6: H's

Happiness

"I accept responsibility for my own happiness"

Happiness is defined as a mental or emotional state of well-being defined by positive or pleasant emotions ranging from contentment to intense joy.

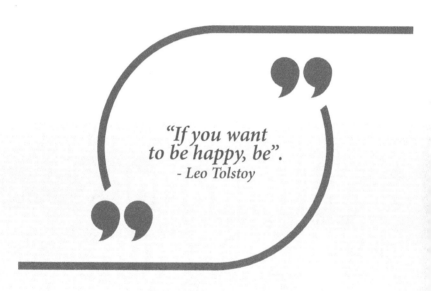

"If you want to be happy, be".
- Leo Tolstoy

Neuroscience now proves that our thoughts can change the structure and function of our brains. When practiced deliberately and repeatedly, they reinforce chemical pathways in the brain, strengthening neural connections. The key is repetition, so you flood your brain with the positive thought. Happiness is not based on what we have, the titles we hold, where we are. Happiness is determined by our attitude toward life. Happiness is determined by our attitude toward life. It is a sense of appreciation for the blessings you have, a realization that you are valuable just as you are. Happiness is within us.

Although, not everyone is born with a happy disposition, but experts say that we can be trained to be happy. There are many ways we can train our mind in happiness. For example, we can choose loving thoughts, words, and actions. The more we practice being in a positive state, the more we will become a vibrant source of happiness we will become a vibrant source of happiness.

Make happiness affirmations part of your healthy life.
- I am free to create my OWN reality. I have choices in all situations.
- My life overflows with happiness and love.
- I choose to release disappointments and everything that no longer add value to my life in return to receive pleasure.
- I am in charge of my own happiness. I let go of the belief that I need someone to "make" me happy.
- Happiness is contagious. I spread happiness to others and absorb happiness from others.
- I am choosing to surround myself with positive, happy people in my life.
- I am a better person each day.

Health

"The greatest wealth is health".

Health is the condition of being sound in body, mind, or spirit.

"The part can never be well unless the whole is well".
- Plato

Good health can be described as the condition where both our bodies, as well as our minds are functioning properly. The main causes behind poor health conditions are diseases, improper diet, injury, mental stress, lack of exercise, unhealthy lifestyle, etc. A person who is fit both physically and mentally is strong enough to face the ups and downs of life and is not affected by drastic changes if they take place. If a person is physically fit, but mentally unwell or troubled, he or she will not be able to function optimally. Being physically healthy means regular physical activity, good nutrition, and adequate rest.

Sleep also plays a vital role in good health and well-being throughout your life. Getting enough quality sleep at the right times can help protect your mental health, physical health, quality of life, and safety. Sleep helps your brain prepare for the next day. It's forming new pathways to help you learn and remember information.

Because our body and mind are connected, one affects the other and vice versa. To be mentally healthy it includes the quality of how you think, feel, and behave and function in daily life. It also affects your ability to cope with stress, overcome challenges, build relationships, and recover from life's setbacks and hardships. Mental fitness can be achieved if your body is functioning well. You can help relax your mind and eliminate stresses by exercising regularly and eating right. The important thing is to know that you have control over your health to make a positive and lasting difference to your well-being.

Here are a few healthy affirmations:
- I treat my body as a temple. It is holy, and it is full of goodness.
- I breathe deeply, exercise regularly and feed only good nutritious food to my body.
- My body is healthy; my mind is brilliant; my soul is tranquil
- My body has a remarkable capacity for healing.
- I pay attention to what my body needs for health and vitality.

CHAPTER 15:

Affirmations Boot Camp Segment #7: I's

Inner Peace

"I AM Peaceful and Will Continuously Seek Peace"

Inner peace refers to a state of being mentally and spiritually at peace, with enough knowledge and understanding to keep oneself strong in the face of discord or stress. Being "at peace" is considered by many to be healthy (homoeostasis) and the opposite of being stressed or anxious. Peace of mind is generally associated with bliss, happiness and contentment.

"Peace is not a relationship of nations. It is a condition of mind brought about by a serenity of soul...

Lasting peace can come only to peaceful people."
- *Jawaharal Nehru*

In a world where stress, worries, fears, noise, and restlessness, inner peace is of paramount importance. It is a treasure that everyone needs, but many people found it hard to find it. Inner peace is the result of a quiet mind. An inner quietness that allows you to see yourself and the world around you as it is, without any aggression, desires, frustration or stress you can feel, simply just to be. People who achieve this inner quietness generally show kindness towards all living things and a deep appreciation for the natural world around them. They see the beauty in everyone and everything. Achieving inner peace is important to living a stable lifestyle and enjoying yourself in whatever you set out to accomplish.

Many people struggle through life unconsciously accepting our thoughts. We simply do not look at or challenge them as they appear. By accepting them, we give them permission to shape our beliefs about ourselves and our lives. Imagine how your life would change, if you could stop dwelling on problems, hurts and wrongs.

During still and peaceful moments, you gain more clarity for your life and take the path of less resistance. Believing we are loved comes with knowing who we are, not judging ourselves or others for mistakes we make, and from daily meditation, in which we feel the unconditional love of God Developing more peace in your life will attract similar energies into your life to include your relationships, career, and health. Give yourself the ability to gain peace and live peacefully. The most beautiful part is being present now, where acceptance is in each moment as it happens.

Affirmations to peaceful existence:
- I grant myself peace within my own mind.
- I bring Peace into moments of chaos and frustrations.
- My Peace is dependent on my thoughts and actions.
- My life is for living, not for worry or doubt,
- Slowly and Deeply, I Inhale a Calming Breath.
- I am healthy and whole and vibrant.

CHAPTER 16:

Affirmations Boot Camp Segment #8: L's

Love

"Love is attracted to me, and I AM attracted to Love ."

It can refer to an emotion of a strong desire, attraction and personal attachment.

"The best love is the kind that awakens the soul; that makes us reach for more, that plants the fire in our hearts and brings peace to our minds.

That's what I hope to give you forever."
~The Notebook

Love is an incredibly powerful emotion a human being can experience. Love is express through actions and words. Love should be experienced and not just felt. Love does not come with conditions, stipulations, addenda, or codes. Like the sun, love radiates independently of our fears and desires.

The part I find most interesting in this definition is the conditions that make love more powerful. First, you can't love someone if you don't love yourself. What exactly does that mean and how does it work? How can you give something you are not familiar with? In order to receive more love, you are to be loving beginning with yourself, where you are setting the blueprint for others to follow.

The meaning of love will change with each person and how they define love. However, true love is constant and consistent. You may have relationships with people who has hurt you, betrayed you, etc. However, remember that love is not responsible for the pain, but the people, who have forgotten the meaning of love.

Furthermore, feelings can be deceptive. Sometimes, what we perceive as love may in fact be another emotion. But actions cannot be mistaken. So, rather than ask, "What is love?" we must ask, "Do I perform acts of love for my beloved?" and "Does my beloved perform acts of love for me?" Everything seems brighter, happier and more wonderful when you're in love. When you find it, cherish it.

Love your way through life using these affirmations:
• Love surrounds me every day in every way.
• I naturally attract loving relationships into my life.
• I effortlessly radiate positive and loving energy.
• I release the past and let love flow into my life.
• I am in a loving and supportive relationship.
• I radiate pure, unconditional love inside out.

CHAPTER 17:

Affirmations Boot Camp Segment #9: P's

Parenting

"I'M Chosen To Guide Productive and Spiritual Being(s)"

Parenting is a supporting the physical, emotional, social, financial, and intellectual development of a child from infancy to adulthood.

> *"At the end of the day, the most overwhelming key to a child's success is the positive involvement of parents."*
> - Jane D. Hull

Raising happy, healthy children is one of the most challenging jobs as parents. No parent is proficient with all parenting skills all the time. Instead, it is a work in progress. Children don't come with a parenting manual, and there's no course that teaches the necessary skills to become effective parents. Parents and caregivers role are to ensure our children are healthy, safe, and equip with the skills and resources they will need to succeed as adults. Experienced parents will tell you how much hard work and dedication goes into it.

Some parents don't approach parenting with the same focus and use the same parenting skills their parents used, whether or not these were effective parenting skills. A parent's relationship with his or her child will be reflected in the child's actions. For example, if you don't have a good relationship with your child, they're not going to listen to you. Think how you relate to other adults. If you have a good relationship with them, you tend to trust them more, listen to their opinions, and agree with them. If it's someone we just don't like, we will ignore their opinion.

We know that our thoughts shape our life. Parents have a strong influence over their children development. They imitate your actions, your attitudes, even your language. So, having good, positive thoughts, attitudes, and actions are vital to shaping your children's choices and directions in life.

However, when your children began to get older, they become influence by other relatives, their peers, media, etc. It is especially important that parents give children a good start, and provide children with a crossing point to the world that eventually prepares them for independence. Positive feelings like self-acceptance or self-confidence help kids try new challenges, cope with mistakes, and become driven.

When kids feel accepted and understood by a parent, they are likely to see themselves in a positive light and accept themselves, also. It also set them up for achievements in other areas in life to include school, friendships, etc. Practicing positive affirmations will improve your confidence in your parenting skills. Use parent affirmations to better care for your children and give them the best version of yourself. Here are our positive parenting affirmations.

The following parent affirmations will serve the purpose.
- I am in-tune to my children's needs.
- I set an excellent example for my kids.
- I am becoming a better parent by the day.
- I am a confident, smart, loving parent.
- I love my children for who they are.
- I am a patient parent, who teaches love, peace, giving and gratitude to my children.
- I continuously grow in my parenting role and acquire effective parenting skills.

Procrastination

"I 'M Here To Create An Abundant Life and Will Waste No Time Doing So"

Procrastination is the avoidance of doing a task which needs to be accomplished. It is the practice of doing more pleasurable things in place of less pleasurable ones or carrying out less urgent tasks instead of more urgent ones, thus putting off impending tasks to a later time. Sometimes, procrastination takes place until the "last minute" before a deadline.

"You don't have to be great to start, but you have to start to be great."
- Zig Ziglar

To sum it up, you procrastinate when you put off things that you should be focusing on right now, usually in favor of doing something that is more enjoyable or that you're more comfortable doing. Procrastination is a habit and deeply ingrained pattern of behavior. That means that you won't just break it overnight. The key idea is that procrastinating does not mean doing absolutely nothing. Procrastinators do absolutely nothing; they do marginally useful things, like sharpening pencils or making a chart of how they will reorganize their files when they get around to it. Many procrastinators overestimate the unpleasantness of a task. So give it a try! You may find that it's not as bad as you thought! Habits only stop being habits when you have persistently stopped practicing them, so use as many approaches as possible to maximize your chances of beating them.

These general tips will help motivate you to get moving: Make up your own rewards. For example, promise yourself a treat at lunchtime if you've completed a certain task. And, make sure you notice how good it feels to finish things! You can ask someone else to check up on you. Peer pressure works! This is the principle behind slimming and other self-help groups, and it is widely recognized as a highly effective approach. Identify the unpleasant consequences of not doing the task. Break the project into a set of smaller, more manageable tasks. You may find it helpful to create an action plan. Start with some quick, small tasks if you can, even if these aren't the logical first actions. You'll feel that you're achieving things, and so perhaps the whole project won't be so overwhelming after all.

Some tips will work better for some people than for others and for some tasks than others. And, sometimes, you may simply need to try a fresh approach to beat the "procrastination danger"! The key when saying, and reading, affirmations, is to feel the feelings they portray. It can help to fully relax and know that at the core of your being, these statements are true.

You can start with these affirmations below.
- I am organized, efficient, productive and proud of all my accomplishment.
- I have the skills, resources and energy to get my to-do list done.
- I choose to focus on the rewards of accomplishing my most pressing projects.
- I take action now and leave the outcome to God!
- I find myself accomplishing more and more, day by day.
- This is the time. This is the place. I am the one. I will act now.

CHAPTER 18:

Affirmations Boot Camp Segment #10: R's

Relationships

"I AM My People's Keeper"

Relationship is the way in which two or more people, groups, countries, etc., talk to, behave toward, and deal with each other: a romantic or sexual friendship between two people: the way in which two or more people or things are connected.

"How people treat you is their karma; how you react is yours".
- Wayne Dyer

Healthy relationships are a very important factor of our health and wellbeing. We are biologically wired to seek close and ongoing connections. Because love is one of the most powerful energy in the universe; as you learn to love yourself and love other people unconditionally you will be attract nothing but great things into your life. There is compelling evidence that strong relationships contribute to a long and happy life. Each of us enters into a romantic relationship or attract friendships with ideas and the relational models based on we witnessed in our childhood and family, what we've seen and heard in the media, and our own history of past relationships experiences.

The Law of Attraction is very simple and straightforward. You attract what you believe. You attract love by being a magnet of love. The people you attract are the reflection of who you are unresolved wounds and lacking within us. If you are loving, cheerful, or positive, you will attract that kind of people into your life. If you are angry, negative, or mistrustful, you are more likely to attract that into your life. Holding on to unrealistic expectations can cause a relationship to be unsatisfying and to fail eventually.

Most of us believe that our relationships will become better if our partners change. When you need another person to change, you place your power on something outside of you. If another must change in order for you to be happy, or in order to have the freedom to do certain things in life is a place of disempowerment. This is not a powerful action of someone who wants to direct the course of his or her life.

Look around at your circumstances. They are a direct result of your belief system and actions. You have the power to create something better and greater. If you are in a relationship, the emotional connection you and your partner share occur in part from your ability to affirm and validate one another. There are many ways to affirm your partner.

It includes in how you say something, the way you interact and touch him/her.

We all affirm our partners, sometimes without realizing the messages we are sending. Creating affirmations helps you to focus on the positive and loving part of your relationship and connection with the person. Successful long-term relationships involve ongoing efforts to do what it takes to improve conditions within your relationships. Use the following affirmations to help create the shift, without causing resistance.

Here are a few affirmations towards helping you be in sync with building the relationship(s) you desired.

• I attract genuine, positive and healthy people.
• I deserve to have a meaningful & spiritual connection with _____.
• No one can harm or diminish the truth of who I am.
• I participate and attract good experience & things to my relationships.
• I inspire others & others inspire me to live a life of wholeness, harmony and meaning.
• I forgave the past and chose to move forward with love and appreciation.

CHAPTER 19:

Affirmations Boot Camp Segment #11: S's

Self-Worth

"I AM A Reflection of Love"

Self-worth is the opinion you have about yourself and the value you place on yourself.

> *"Never be bullied into silence. Never allow yourself to be made a victim. Accept no one's definition of your life, but define yourself."*
> *- Harvey Fierstein*

Self-worth is what enables us to believe that we are capable of being and doing our best and contributing well in society. How you perceive yourself, how you talk about yourself, and how you represent yourself eventually becomes a reality for you. Self-worth is frequently based on our feelings of worth in terms of our skills, achievements, status, financial resources, or physical attributes, in which is misguided.

When we find ourselves not measuring up to other people expectations and society's criteria, we suffer. Self-worth is more spiritually connected, as it is directly related to your existence and overall feeling of importance and value in this world

Having self worth means you establish healthy boundaries, and prioritize your needs and assume the responsibility to value and care for yourself instead assigning the job to someone else. Feeling worthy does equip you with the skills to identify what you want and what you deserve to have, and the strength to disconnect from anything that dishonor you. People with high self worth know their value and know they are good and lovable and understand the right people will also view them the same way. People who know their worth don't have to question how someone sees them because they live by their own definition of value. They also know if a relationship ended it's not because something was wrong with them, but the relationship served its purpose, and they take the lessons the relationship came to taught them.

The pursuit of worthiness and approval drives us steadily farther from being in peace and feeling whole. If you want to end the feelings of unworthiness, then own them. You created the feelings, and you can change them. Accepting who you are positively changes your life. Your worthiness is not based on your weaknesses, limitations, and imperfections. Those things should in no way interferes with your ability to fully accept yourself because no one is perfect and most importantly, you were birth in the image of our creator, who makes you worthy.

Affirmations promoting self worth:

- I am able to forgive myself when I make mistakes.
- I have love and compassion for myself and others.
- Every day I grow emotionally stronger
- I grant myself the Honor of being ME.
- I am worthy of all the best that life has to offer
- I do not need anyone's permission to be my true self.
- I choose to see all difficulties as opportunities to make me stronger.

Spirituality

"I AM a Spiritual Vessel "

Spirituality is relating to, consisting of, or having the nature of spirit; not material; supernatural.

"Just as a candle cannot burn without fire, men cannot live without a spiritual life."
- Buddha

Spirituality is a broad concept and means something different to everyone. Spirituality is also used as a way of gaining perspective, that our role in life has a greater value. Spirituality is a sense of connection to something bigger than ourselves, which can result in positive emotions, such as peace, happiness, gratitude, and acceptance. Spirituality may also describe for some people their connection to each other and themselves. We commonly express our spirituality by going to church, synagogue, a mosque, etc. And other reach higher levels of consciousness through private prayer, meditation, art, quiet reflection, etc.

Spirituality as a great way we seek solace and peace in our lives and as a way of coping with change or uncertainty. Spirituality starts as a small seed and grows with time and experience. It leads someone to strive for a state of harmony with oneself and others while working to balance inner needs with the rest of the world. It can separate a person from dependence on the material aspect of the world and establish a greater purpose, which is often expressed as intimacy with God.Loving and respecting all religions and images of God doesn't mean that you have to agree with all their doctrines. This goes for any teachings you may encounter along your path. Everybody is doing something different, and each one believes deep in his soul that what he/she believes is right. By clarifying what's most important, you can focus less on the unimportant things and eliminate stressors in your life.

The next time you are out in nature, pay attention to how everything is connected. Everything flows naturally and easily, even when the conditions are harsh. This is the simple truth that we are not separate from each other or from the earth. Everything works together harmoniously. Cultivating spirituality greatly contributes to our overall joy and happiness. It's never too late to develop it further and enjoy the benefits it brings.

Here are a few affirmations for the soul:
- God's love is working with me now and always.
- I radiate my kindness into the world.
- I see the miracle in all of life.
- I am a magnificent gift to the world.
- I open myself to receive the flow of the spirit.
- The love of God flows through me. We are one.
- I am grateful for all I am, have, give and receive.
- I'm a magnificent reflection of the great Devine,

CHAPTER 20:

Affirmations Boot Camp Segment #12: W's

Weight Loss

"I AM In Control of What I Put In My Temple"

Weight loss refers to a reduction of the total body mass, due to a loss of fluid, body fat. The loss may be the result of a change in diet or life-style or a febrile disease.

"Successful weight loss takes programming, not willpower".
- *Phil McGraw*

Your weight can be a balancing act. To lose weight, you need to burn more calories than you eat and drink. Some factors such as your age, genes, medicines, and lifestyle habits may affect your weight. If you would like to use positive affirmations to help you lose weight, speak only positive words, describing what you really want. Avoid telling yourself "I am fat"; as this is a negative statement of what you do not want. Say instead, "I am getting slimmer" Or, "I'm working towards my ideal healthy weight".

Doing so will bring forth positive images in mind to help you reach your weight and health goals.

Consult with your health care provider about factors that may affect your weight. The key to successful weight loss is a commitment to making indefinite changes in your diet and exercise habits and being mentally and emotionally prepared will help you stay focus towards achieving your weight goals.

Here are a few affirmations to help you get in the right mindset towards your weight loss goals.

- I appreciate and love my body and mind unconditionally.
- I am delighted to be the ideal weight for me.
- Living a healthy lifestyle is becoming easier.
- I am becoming more disciplined with each passing day.
- I make good and healthy eating choices based on my nourishment needs.
- I'm in control of my body and have excellent health.
- I have healthy eating habits to strengthen my body.

CHAPTER 21:

Shift Your Life Activities

You create your own opportunities.

It is helpful to understand how our thoughts,

feelings and behaviors are linked.

Cognitive Triangle

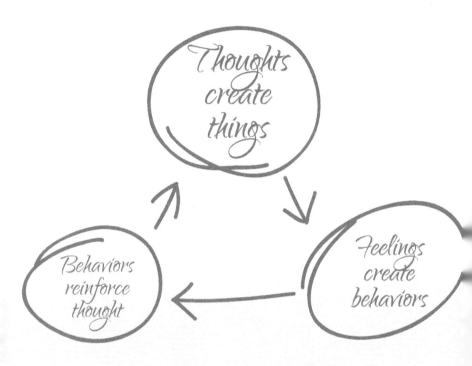

Cognitive Behavior Therapy (CBT) was developed from clinical work conducted by Dr. Aaron T. Beck, a psychiatrist, and Albert Ellis, a psychologist.

Get Tuned In

Exercise: #1

Directions: Answer the questions below and reflect on your responses.

1) Write your most dominating thoughts below.

Example: I sometimes worry and think about how I'm going to pay my bills.

a.

b.

c.

2) Write the feelings associated with the dominate thoughts.

Example: I often feel anxious when I think about my finance.

a.

b.

c.

3) How do you behave when these dominate thoughts and feelings occur?

Example: When I feel anxious I began to eat more.

a.

b.

c.

If you don't like what you are producing, what can you do to shift the cycle you are currently in, and produce more of what you want?

Examples are below:

1. Thoughts
I can think about the obstacles I overcame in my life to remind me of my strength.

2. Feelings
I will intentional decide to feel grateful for the experiences I encounter.

3. Actions
I will get more rest and exercise to help me reduce my anxiety.

Empower Yourself

Exercise: #2

Directions: Write and complete on a separate sheet of paper.

List negative thoughts and/or feelings you have about yourself	List why these thoughts are not true	List positive thoughts and feelings that can replace the negative ones	List actions you can take to support your positive thoughts
Examples: I think that I don't have what it takes to open a business.	I haven't listed and take a closer look at all of my skill sets and talents.	I am enough and I have enough to get started.	I will identify talent(s) and resources that I have. I will develop it, use it, and share it with others.

Affirming Your Life

Exercise: #3

Directions: Write down affirmations that you identify strongly with and will help empower you to overcome your challenging areas. Spend at least 10 minutes every day thinking about your goals and what you want from life. Say your affirmations repeatedly and visualize what you want.

Examples: I'm wonderfully made and with a purpose.	My Finances are increasing each and every day, as I find more income streams.	My health gets better and I choose to exercise 3 days a week and eat healthier.

Affirmation(s) Tips

• Make a gratitude list of people and things you are thankful for. Doing so will draw more good things into your life that you can be grateful for.

• Write down what you want to see happen. However, embrace where you are in order to get to your desires more easily. Remember, if you don't like where are, but you make peace with it, you will prevent it from blocking your manifestation process.

• Use a picture of what you want and post it in a visible area(s). You can create a vision board or post pictures and words to help you see and feel what you desire. You can leave empowering notes for yourself to read.

• You must act, speak, and think as if you already received it.

• Meditate, pray and do activities that embrace the process.

• Be faithful in your pursuit despite how long it takes to manifest your dream life.

CHAPTER 22:

Empower U Corner:
Life-Changing Thoughts to Practice Daily

Failure

Success

"The line between failure and success is so fine that we scarcely
know when we pass it - so fine that we often are on the line
and do not know it."

- Ralph Waldo

I am a miracle and one of a kind.

(Provide supporting reasons that makes this statement true.)

_____

_____

_____

_____

_____

_____

_____

_____

_____

_____

I am a remarkable human being!

(Provide supporting reasons that makes this statement true.)

_____

_____

_____

_____

_____

_____

_____

_____

_____

_____

I'm worthy and more than enough.

(Provide supporting reasons that makes this statement true.)

_____

_____

_____

_____

_____

_____

_____

_____

_____

_____

I was created on purpose and for a purpose.

(Provide supporting reasons that makes this statement true.)

_____

_____

_____

_____

_____

_____

_____

_____

_____

_____

_____

Yes, I can do it!

(Provide supporting reasons that makes this statement true.)

_____

_____

_____

_____

_____

_____

_____

_____

_____

_____

_____

Greatness lives within me.

(Provide supporting reasons that makes this statement true.)

_____

_____

_____

_____

_____

_____

_____

_____

_____

_____

I'm a powerful force!

(Provide supporting reasons that makes this statement true.)

_____

_____

_____

_____

_____

_____

_____

_____

_____

_____

I overcame….

(List challenges and barriers that you have overcame
in your life. Sometimes, you may need to be reminded
of how strong you are.)

_____

_____

_____

_____

_____

_____

_____

_____

_____

_____

_____

I am thankful for....

(List reasons that makes this statement true.)

_____

_____

_____

_____

_____

_____

_____

_____

_____

_____

I'm unstoppable!

(Provide supporting reasons that makes this statement true.)

_____

_____

_____

_____

_____

_____

_____

_____

_____

_____

_____

I AM....

(Fill in empowering statements using the phrase above.)

_____

_____

_____

_____

_____

_____

_____

_____

_____

_____

_____

I'm Unstoppable

How to Use Affirmations to Shape Your
Reality and Achieve Success.

_____

_____

_____

_____

_____

_____

_____

_____

_____

_____

My Life Goals

Directions: Write down your goals for each time period.

This week:
_____

This month:
_____

In six (6)months:
_____

In one (1) year:
_____

My Life Goals Affirmation and Action Plans

Directions: Write down the action(s) and affirmations you will take to support the goals you have identified and written.

1. This week:
_____

2. This month:
_____

3. In six (6)months:
_____

4. One (1) year:
_____

Author's Corner

Florence Gaspard is a dynamic speaker, success coach and entrepreneur. Her platform includes the area of personal and professional development. She is passionate about helping others learn how to overcome challenges in their lives and materialize a better quality of life by achieving their targeted goals. Her purpose is to connect with people through their difficult circumstances by offering tools and strategies that are simple, practical and energy efficient for the best outcomes in their lives.

Holding degrees in both Psychology and Mental Health Counseling, Florence's credentials and talent has allow her gain success in both personal and business development. Her experiences involved both for profit and non-profit settings. Having this versatility allowed her the flexibility to adapt to the various environment and worked with diverse backgrounds. Florence's expanding platform also allows her to connect to a broader reach of audiences through a range of media outlets including several appearances on local and national radio broadcast stations and televised programs. In addition to being a well-liked motivational speaker and coach, Florence has authored well-received books written for both adults and children. Contact Florence to identify how she can help you began to transform your life.

For more information about Florence and her services
and products visit www.florencegaspard.com